Collins
INTERNATIONAL
PRIMARY
ENGLISH

Progress Book 2

Student's Book

William Collins' dream of knowledge for all began with the publication of his first book in 1819.
A self-educated mill worker, he not only enriched millions of lives, but also founded a flourishing publishing house.
Today, staying true to this spirit, Collins books are packed with inspiration, innovation and practical expertise.
They place you at the centre of a world of possibility and give you exactly what you need to explore it.

Collins. Freedom to teach.

Published by Collins

An imprint of HarperCollins*Publishers*
The News Building, 1 London Bridge Street, London, SE1 9GF, UK

HarperCollins*Publishers*
Macken House, 39/40 Mayor Street Upper, Dublin 1, D01 C9W8, Ireland

Browse the complete Collins catalogue at
www.collins.co.uk

© HarperCollins*Publishers* Limited 2023

10 9 8 7 6 5 4 3 2 1

ISBN 978-0-00-865480-1

British Library Cataloguing-in-Publication Data
A catalogue record for this publication is available from the British Library.

Author: Daphne Paizee
Series editor: Daphne Paizee
Publisher: Elaine Higgleton
Product manager: Holly Woolnough
Project manager: Just Content
Copy editor: Tanya Solomons
Proofreader: Catherine Dakin
Cover designer: Gordon MacGilp
Cover illustration: David Roberts
Typesetter: David Jimenez
Illustrator: Ann Paganuzzi
Production controller: Lyndsey Rogers
Printed and bound in Great Britain by Martins the Printers

With thanks to the following teachers for reviewing materials in proof and providing valuable feedback: Sylvie Meurein, Nilai International School; Gabriel Kehinde, Avi-Cenna International School; and with thanks to the following teachers who provided feedback during the early development stage: Najihah binti Roslan, Nilai International School.

MIX
Paper | Supporting
responsible forestry
FSC
www.fsc.org **FSC™ C007454**

Contents

How to use this book

This book is full of questions. Each set of questions can be completed at the end of each week.

The questions allow you to practise the things you've learned. They will help you understand topics that you might need more practice of. They will also show you the topics that you are most confident with. Your teacher can use your answers to give you feedback and support.

At the end of each set of questions, there is a space to put the date that you completed it. There is also a blank box. Your teacher might use it to:

- sign, when they have marked your answers
- write a short comment on your work.

Date: _____

Now look at and think about each of the *I can* statements.

Pages 5 to 11 include a list of *I can* statements. Once you have finished each set of questions, turn to the *I can* statements. Think about each statement: how easy or hard did you find the topic? For each statement, colour in the face that is closest to how you feel:

☺ I can do this   😐 I'm getting there   ☹ I need some help.

There are three longer termly tests in the book. These can be completed after each block of units.

I can statements

At the end of each week, think about each of the *I can* statements and how easy or hard you find the topic. For each statement, colour in the face that is closest to how you feel.

Unit 1 Fun and games	Date:		
Week 1			
I can read a story aloud and act it.	☺	😐	☹
I can write and answer questions about the story.	☺	😐	☹
Week 2			
I can read and spell new words using spelling patterns.	☺	😐	☹
I can make lists.	☺	😐	☹
I can write my own story.	☺	😐	☹
Week 3			
I can read a poem aloud and talk about it.	☺	😐	☹
I can find rhyming words in a poem.	☺	😐	☹
I can make sentences interesting.	☺	😐	☹
Unit 2 The Olympics	Date:		
Week 1			
I can read information and answer questions.	☺	😐	☹
I can write words that rhyme.	☺	😐	☹
I can give information in drawings and writing.	☺	😐	☹

Week 2			
I can read and talk about information on a poster.	☺	😐	☹
I can read and spell words using spelling patterns.	☺	😐	☹
I can make a glossary for a book.	☺	😐	☹
Week 3			
I can find information on a chart.	☺	😐	☹
I can write about events.	☺	😐	☹
I can talk about instructions.	☺	😐	☹
Unit 3 Creatures great and small	Date:		
Week 1			
I can read a story with pictures and answer questions.	☺	😐	☹
I can read long words and new words.	☺	😐	☹
I can talk about a story.	☺	😐	☹
Week 2			
I can write plural words and verbs that end in -ed and -ing.	☺	😐	☹
I can put sentences in order to tell a story.	☺	😐	☹
I can find information about a farm animal and present this information.	☺	😐	☹
Week 3			
I can spell words with long vowel sounds.	☺	😐	☹
I can read a poem and talk about it.	☺	😐	☹
I can use adjectives to describe an animal.	☺	😐	☹

Term 1 Test			
I can read a story and answer questions about it.	☺	😐	☹
I can write about an animal.	☺	😐	☹
I can complete sentences.	☺	😐	☹
Unit 4 _Kind Emma_	**Date:**		
Week 1			
I can read aloud fluently and with expression.	☺	😐	☹
I can use capital letters and full stops in sentences.	☺	😐	☹
I can find and understand pronouns.	☺	😐	☹
I can make sentences with 'and'.	☺	😐	☹
Week 2			
I can write new words that begin with _un-_, _dis-_ and _re-_.	☺	😐	☹
I can find and use verbs in sentences.	☺	😐	☹
I can work out what a character feels from what they say.	☺	😐	☹
Week 3			
I can retell a story.	☺	😐	☹
I can use 'and' and 'if' in sentences.	☺	😐	☹
I can describe the time when something happens.	☺	😐	☹
I can plan and write a story and check for errors.	☺	😐	☹

Unit 5 Animals and us	Date:		
Week 1			
I can listen to and answer questions about a poem.	☺	😐	☹
I can read stories from different times and places.	☺	😐	☹
I can explain what words mean and pronounce words correctly.	☺	😐	☹
Week 2			
I can read and spell words with *-ful, -ph*.	☺	😐	☹
I can spell words that sound the same but have different meanings.	☺	😐	☹
I can write sentences about a story.	☺	😐	☹
Week 3			
I can tell the difference between fiction and non-fiction.	☺	😐	☹
I can put words in alphabetical order.	☺	😐	☹
I can write a story.	☺	😐	☹
Unit 6 Staying safe	**Date:**		
Week 1			
I can read and answer questions about a contents page.	☺	😐	☹
I can read information and write answers to questions.	☺	😐	☹
I can complete sentences with the correct vocabulary.	☺	😐	☹

Week 2			
I can read and answer questions about a chart.	☺	😐	☹
I can write and count syllables in words.	☺	😐	☹
I can use information to complete a chart.	☺	😐	☹
I can do a presentation of information.	☺	😐	☹
Week 3			
I can find words that rhyme.	☺	😐	☹
I can write sentences with punctuation marks.	☺	😐	☹
I can talk about and describe dangers.	☺	😐	☹
Term 2 Test			
I can read a contents page.	☺	😐	☹
I can read non-fiction text and answer questions about the information.	☺	😐	☹
I can compile a chart.	☺	😐	☹
I can write a book review.	☺	😐	☹
Unit 7 If	**Date:**		
Week 1			
I can read part of a poem aloud and answer questions about it.	☺	😐	☹
I can write sentences.	☺	😐	☹
I can write words in alphabetical order.	☺	😐	☹

Week 2			
I can write sentences correctly.	😊	😐	☹️
I can recognise and use nouns, adjectives and verbs in sentences.	😊	😐	☹️
Week 3			
I can read and spell words that rhyme.	😊	😐	☹️
I can write sentences with 'and', 'but' and 'because'.	😊	😐	☹️
I can interview someone and write a report.	😊	😐	☹️
Unit 8 *The Pot of Gold*	**Date:**		
Week 1			
I can read part of a story aloud fluently.	😊	😐	☹️
I can answer questions about a story.	😊	😐	☹️
I can draw and describe a character using interesting adjectives.	😊	😐	☹️
Week 2			
I can retell a story with events in the correct order.	😊	😐	☹️
I can write plural forms and compound words.	😊	😐	☹️
I can use connecting words in sentences.	😊	😐	☹️
I can write direct speech.	😊	😐	☹️

Week 3			
I can write questions and use question marks.	☺	😐	☹
I can use interesting words to describe a character.	☺	😐	☹
I can tell a story with a new ending.	☺	😐	☹
Unit 9 People who help us	Date:		
Week 1			
I can read and find information in non-fiction texts.	☺	😐	☹
I can work out what words mean in a text.	☺	😐	☹
Week 2			
I can make compound words.	☺	😐	☹
I can find syllables in words.	☺	😐	☹
I can talk about and write important pieces of information.	☺	😐	☹
Week 3			
I can read indexes and glossaries.	☺	😐	☹
I can answer questions about firefighting.	☺	😐	☹
I can write full sentences.	☺	😐	☹
Term 3 Test			
I can read a text aloud and talk about it.	☺	😐	☹
I can read a new story and answer questions about it.	☺	😐	☹

1 Read aloud part of the story *Jodie the Juggler.*

Jodie went to Asif's flat.

Jodie showed Asif how to juggle.

They juggled with Asif's socks.

They juggled with Asif's shoes.

They juggled with three apples and ...

... they broke a plate.

"Boys," said Asif's dad, "go outside and play football."

Jodie didn't want to play football. He wanted to juggle.

2   Answer the questions.

   a   Where are Jodie and Asif?

   _____

   b   What did they juggle? Make a list of three nouns.

   _____

   _____

   _____

   c   Who said, "Hello Jodie, come on in."?

   _____

   d   What do you think Jodie said when they broke the plate? Look at the third picture.

   _____

   e   How was Asif's dad feeling when he said, "Boys, go outside and play football." Choose a word and write a sentence with the word.

   unhappy   excited   frightened

   _____

3   Write questions about the story. Start like this:

Who _____

What _____

Where _____

Ask a partner to answer the questions.

4   Act the part of the story that you read. Use your voice and your body to show how the characters are feeling.

Look at and think about each of the *I can* statements.

Date: _____

1 Write a word to name each picture.

2 🎧 Audio 1 Listen and write the sentences that you hear.

a _____

b _____

c _____

d _____

e _____

3 Circle each word in these compound words.

(foot)(ball)   grandfather   teaspoon   skateboard
supermarket   upstairs   rainbow

4 What did Jodie break? Write these words in a list in two different ways.

cup   plate   eggs   flowerpots   glass

cup, _____

cup

_____   _____

_____   _____

5 What happened when Jodie started to play football? Write your own story. Start like this:

The next day, Jodie said, "I want to _____

_____

_____

Continue your story in your notebook.

Look at and think about each of the *I can* statements.

Date: _____

15

1 Read the poem aloud.

A Little Bird

I saw a blue bird
Go hop, hop, hop.
I said, "Little blue bird,
Will you stop, stop, stop?"

Then I was going to the window
To say, "How do you do?"
But he chirped "Tweet, tweet",
And away he flew!

2 Answer the questions.

a Find the words in the poem that rhyme.

hop _____

do _____

b Write two words that suggest the sound the bird makes.

_____   _____

c What did the blue bird do? Tick two sentences.

☐ It chirped and flew away.

☐ It hopped on the windowsill.

☐ It shouted "Stop!"

3 Talk with a partner about the poem.

• Does the person who wrote the poem like birds?

• How do you think the person felt when the bird flew away?

• How do you think the bird felt?

4 Complete the sentences. Add a word to each sentence to make it more interesting.

a Janice juggled with _____ jellybeans.

b I love your _____ T-shirt.

c Zara is riding a _____ skateboard

d He likes the shoes with _____ shoelaces.

5 Choose a word from the box to describe a sound in each sentence.

| crashed | zooming | creaked | screeched |

a The plate _____ to the ground!

b Is that a rocket _____ up into the sky?

c The wooden stairs _____ as I walked up them.

d The car _____ to a stop at the red light.

6 Draw a picture using one of the sound words below.

Look at and think about each of the *I can* statements.

Date: _____

1 Draw a picture to match each label.

medal	flag	wreath

2 🎧 Audio 2 Listen and complete each word with *oy* or *oi*.

b __ __   c __ __ n   m __ __ st   ann __ __   sp __ __ l

3 Read the information about the Olympic Games.

Olympic sports

There are many different sporting events in the Olympics. The sports in the Summer Olympics are different from the sports in the Winter Olympics.

snowboarding (winter)

athletics (summer)

New sports

There are also some new sports, such as skateboarding, karate, climbing and surfing.

skateboarding (summer)

surfing (summer)

4 Answer the questions.

   a Name a sport at the Summer Olympics.

   _____

   b Name a sport at the Winter Olympics.

   _____

   c Name two new sports at the Olympics.

   _____   _____

   d Which sport would you like to do?

   _____

5 What is a 'podium' at the Olympic Games? Draw a picture and label it. Then write a sentence with more information about the podium.

_____

Date: _____

Look at and think about each of the *I can* statements.

1 Read the poster and talk with a partner about the information it shows.

Diving at the **Olympic Games Finals**
Venue Olympic Stadium, diving pool
Date 22nd July
Competitors Finalists: women

2 Answer the questions.

a What sport can you see on 22nd July?

_____

b Where can you see the sport?

_____

c Who is competing?

_____

3 Circle six words with the long *u* sound.

glue   games   cube   flew   blue

tea   crew   June   but   moon

4 🎧 Audio 3   Listen and write the sentences that you hear.

a _____

b _____

c _____

d _____

5   Choose the correct word to complete each sentence.

  a The runners line up for the race on the _____ line. (starting, jumping)

  b We _____ about the Olympic Games. (read, reed)

  c Which relay _____ won the gold medal? (team, teem)

  d We will _____ swimming at the Summer Olympics. (sea, see)

6   Put these words in alphabetical order for a glossary. Tell a partner what the words mean.

| competitors   ancient   torch   spectators |

_____

_____

_____

_____

Look at and think about each of the *I can* statements.

Date: _____

21

1 Read the chart. It has information about Olympic medal winners.

2 Complete the sentence.

This chart shows the medals won by some countries at the Olympic

Games in _____

in 20 _____ .

Tokyo Olympics 2020

Country		Gold medals	Silver medals	Bronze medals
Kenya		4	4	2
India		1	2	4
Italy		10	10	20
New Zealand		7	6	7
Spain		3	8	6

3 Write the name of the country for each flag.

_____ _____ _____ _____

4 Answer the questions.

a How many gold medals did Kenya win? _____

b How many bronze medals did India win? _____

c Which country won 10 gold medals and 10 silver medals?

_____

5 Choose either **A** *or* **B**.

A Imagine that you are a spectator at the Olympic Games. Write in your diary about the event.

- Describe what you saw and how you felt.

B Imagine you are a news reporter. Write an article about a school event.

- Explain what the event was about.
- Give your article a headline.

_____

_____

_____

_____

_____

_____

_____

6 Think about something you have made in class, for example, medals or torches. Talk with a partner about the instructions that you used.

- Did the instructions have numbers?
- Did you find the instructions easy to follow?
- Can you give the same instructions to someone else, in order?

Look at and think about each of the *I can* statements.

Date: _____

1 Look at the pictures carefully. Then read the story.

A Different Duckling

A long time ago, a mother duck laid three eggs in a nest. Then she left the eggs to go for a swim. While she was away, a swan laid an egg in her nest.

CRACK! CRACK! CRACK! Three fluffy yellow ducklings hatched. Then the fourth egg hatched. And out popped a scruffy brown duckling. "Quark! Quark!" she said happily.

"You look different," quacked the other ducklings.

Mother duck looked at her and looked at the other ducklings. "Come along then, all of you! Time to learn to swim," she said.

She led the ducks to a nearby pond. They all swam. The scruffy brown duckling swam faster than the others.

The next day, they went for a walk around the farm. The farm animals stared at them.

"You look different," mooed the cow. "You're not yellow."

"Nor are you," replied the scruffy duckling.

"You aren't fluffy," neighed the donkey.

"Nor are you," replied the duckling.

The ducklings grew up together. They ate and swam together. They were good friends.

The scruffy brown duckling grew up and became a big white swan. She went to live with other swans, but she came to visit her friends the ducks every day.

2 Answer the questions about *A Different Duckling*.

a How does it start? Circle the correct answer.

A long time ago   A different duckling

b Is this a story or a text with information?

_____

c Who are the characters?

_____

d How many eggs hatched?

_____

e Find a word in the story that rhymes with 'scruffy'.

_____

f Why did the animals call one duckling 'different'? Tick the correct answer.

☐ She was rude and cheeky.

☐ She was a different colour and she was not fluffy.

3 Read these words from the story aloud and talk about them with a partner.

neighed   mooed   together   different

• How many syllables (parts) are there in each word?

• What do the words mean?

• Make a sentence with each word.

4 Talk about *The Different Duckling* and the fairy tale *The Ugly Duckling*.

• Are they the same? How?

• Do the stories end the same way? Which ending do you like?

Look at and think about each of the *I can* statements. ☐

Date: _____

1 Use the words in the box to complete the sentences. Add -*ed*, -*ing* or make the word plural.

> hatch   learn   goat   goose

a Four ducklings _____ out of the eggs yesterday.

b The ducklings are _____ how to swim in the river.

c There are four _____ on the farm.

d Can you see the three _____ up in the sky?

2 Put these sentences about *The Different Duckling* in order. Write the numbers 1 to 6 in the boxes.

☐ The scruffy duckling became a big white swan.

☐ A swan laid an egg in the duck's nest.

☐ The four ducklings grew up together.

☐ Four eggs hatched, but one duckling looked different.

☐ The ducklings walked around the farm.

☐ The ducklings learned how to swim.

3 Circle the names of the books where you can find out facts about farm animals.

Ducks in a row

The little horse

How to raise farm animals

Goats

SHEEP AND GOATS

4 Do some research on a farm animal.

- Draw a picture of the farm animal.
- Label your picture.
- Write two sentences with facts about the animal.

5 Make a presentation to a partner about the animal you have drawn.

Look at and think about each of the *I can* statements.

Date: _____

1 Write a word to name each picture.

2 🎧 Audio 4 Write the sentences that you hear.

a _____

b _____

c _____

d _____

3 Choose the correct word from the box to complete each sentence.

to   too   two   to

a Ducks have _____ wings.

b The ducklings went down _____ the river to swim.

c What do ducks like _____ eat?

d The mouse is _____ small to see in the long grass.

4 Read the poem silently.
- Tell a partner what it is about.
- Do you like the poem? Say why or why not.

The Fieldmouse
Where the acorn tumbles down,
Where the ash tree sheds its berry,
With your fur so soft and brown,
With your eye so round and merry,
Scarcely moving the long grass,
Fieldmouse, I can see you pass.
by Cecil Frances Alexander

Unit 3 Creatures great and small

5 Find the words in the poem that rhyme with these words.

down: _____

berry: _____

grass: _____

6 Write sentences to describe the fieldmouse. Use words (adjectives) that the poet uses and your own words.

_____

_____

_____

_____

Look at and think about each of the *I can* statements.

Date: _____

29

1 Look at the picture of a page from a book.

Hanako's Egg

Written by Mio Debnam

Illustrated by Yu Kito Lee

Collins

a What is this story about?

_____

b Who wrote the story?

_____

2 Listen to parts 1 and 2 of *Hanako's Egg*.

3   Read part 3 below silently.

3 The hen house

Cheep will soon be a hen.

Hanako puts up a hen house in the back garden for Cheep to sleep in.

Hanako puts fresh bedding in the hen house.

Still no eggs for me?

One morning, Cheep starts clucking.

Buck Buck

Hanako runs to the garden in alarm. Cheep is sitting on the bag Hanako took to the farm.

4 Answer the questions about the story.

   a Tick the sentences that are true.

      ☐ Cheep grows up into a hen.

      ☐ Hanako and her dad make a house for Cheep.

      ☐ Cheep does not like the house.

      ☐ Cheep lays lots of eggs.

      ☐ One morning Hanako hears Cheep making a noise.

   b Look at the last picture in question 3.

     i Where is Cheep? _____

     ii Why was she making a noise? _____

   c What does the word 'bedding' mean?

    _____

   d Write these words to show the syllables.

    garden _____

    clucking _____

   e Find words that rhyme in the story.

    morning _____

    farm _____

5 What will happen next in the story? Write an ending.

_____

_____

_____

_____

6 Tell the whole story to a partner.

7 Choose the correct word to complete each sentence.

a Chicks have _____ wings. (two, too)

b Hanako and her dad are _____ a house for the hen today. (makes, making)

c A chick _____ out of the egg and it grew into a hen. (hatching, hatched)

d Which country won three gold _____ at the Olympic Games? (medal, medals)

e How many _____ can you see at the animal farm? (childs, children)

f The wind is _____ through the leaves of the trees. (whistling, whistles)

8 Write a diary entry about an animal. Use adjectives to describe the animal and say how you feel about it.

_____

_____

_____

_____

_____

_____

_____

Look at and think about each of the *I can* statements.

Date: _____

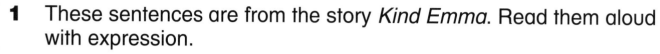

1 These sentences are from the story *Kind Emma*. Read them aloud with expression.

"Come into my house," said Kind Emma.

The little voice said: "I ate long ago. I need food so!"

The floor was scrubbed and the house was tidy and clean.

"Good food and a fire, and someone to talk to! What more could I want?" said Kind Emma.

2 Rewrite the sentences with capital letters and full stops.

a kind emma had no one to talk to

_____

b she opened the door and a tiny thing scuttled in

_____

c she put a dish of hot soup on the table

_____

d the tiny thing stayed hidden it was afraid to come out

_____

3 What did Kind Emma do to help the tiny thing? Write two sentences with 'and'.

_____

_____

4   Use the word 'and' to make sentences and write them below.

Kind Emma opened the door		made fresh bread.
The tiny thing cleaned the house	and	she had someone to talk to.
Kind Emma had good food		a tiny thing scuttled in.
Kind Emma poked the fire		she put some soup on the table.

_____

_____

_____

_____

5   Write each pronoun on the line below. For each one, circle the name of the character they refer to.

"I'll make the fire glow for you," said Kind Emma and she poked the fire. The tiny thing stayed hidden. It was afraid to come out.

I   =   (Kind Emma)   The tiny thing.

_____   =   Kind Emma   The tiny thing

_____   =   Kind Emma   The tiny thing

_____   =   Kind Emma   The tiny thing

Look at and think about each of the *I can* statements.

Date: _____

1 **a** Add prefixes from the box to make new words.

dis-   un-   re-

happy   _____

lock   _____

like   _____

obey   _____

fill   _____

use   _____

b Choose two of the new words you made in question 1 and write your own sentences with the words.

_____

_____

2 🎧 Listen and write the sentences that you hear.
Audio 6

a _____

b _____

c _____

d _____

3 Circle the verbs in the sentences.

a She opened the door for the tiny thing.

b The tiny thing stayed with Kind Emma.

c She put a small spoon on the table.

4 Use the verbs from question 3 in your own sentences.

_____

_____

_____

5 Answer the questions about *Kind Emma*.

  a Tick the sentence that shows Emma was kind.

☐ Next morning, when Emma awoke the fire burned.

☐ "You can share what I have."

  b Tick the sentence that shows the tiny thing was afraid.

☐ The tiny thing stayed hidden.

☐ Fresh bread was ready.

  c Tick the sentence that shows Kind Emma was happy to share her house with the tiny thing.

☐ "What more could I want?" said Kind Emma.

☐ Kind Emma lived alone.

6 Think about how Emma and the tiny thing might act and talk. Act the story of Kind Emma and the tiny thing.

Look at and think about each of the *I can* statements. ☐

Date: _____

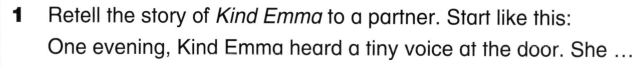

1 Retell the story of *Kind Emma* to a partner. Start like this:

One evening, Kind Emma heard a tiny voice at the door. She …

2 Complete the sentences with 'and' or 'if'.

a "You can share my soup _____ you are hungry," Emma said.

b It is cold outside _____ I am shivering!

c Before dinner, we played football _____ we watched a movie.

d I will go outside later _____ it isn't raining.

3 Use words or phrases from the box to complete the sentences. Each sentence says when something will happen or when it happened.

In the morning	in a few days	then	last week	Tuesday

a I read a good story _____.

b _____ Emma saw that the house was tidy.

c First I made some toast and _____ I warmed up the soup.

d We will go on holiday _____.

e On _____ we visited the Science Museum.

4 Pretend that you meet a small creature. You are kind to the creature.

Plan your story here. Write words or draw a picture in each box.

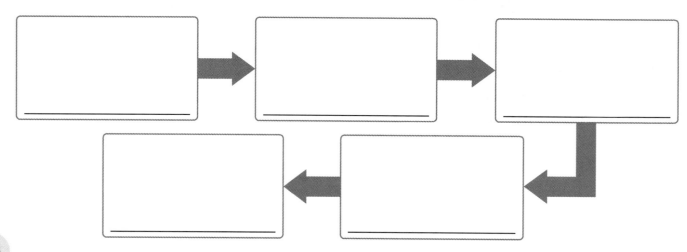

5 Write your story here. Read it aloud and correct any mistakes.

_____

_____

_____

_____

_____

_____

_____

_____

_____

_____

_____

_____

_____

_____

_____

6 Tell a partner about your story.

Look at and think about each of the *I can* statements.

Date: _____

1  Listen to the poem 'Dolphin Ballet' again. Write 'true' or 'false' for each sentence.

a The dolphin is swimming in the water. _____

b The dolphin is a white and silvery blue colour. _____

c The dolphin makes big noisy waves in the water. _____

d The setting of the poem is at night. _____

2 Write a word to name each picture.

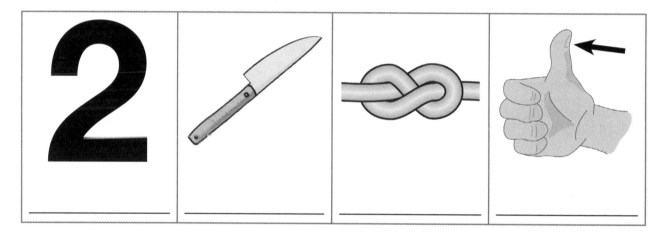

3 Tick the correct meaning of the underlined word in each sentence.

a "You'll all drown!" the knight <u>screamed</u>.

☐ shouted loudly

☐ spoke quietly

b "You must heal him," the knight <u>whispered</u>.

☐ said in a quiet voice

☐ said in a hissing voice

c Jean <u>hurled</u> his spear at the dolphin.

☐ threw forcefully

☐ shouted loudly

d The dolphin <u>dived</u> under the waves.

☐ cried loudly

☐ jumped into the water, head first

4 Read the text from story *The Dolphin King* aloud.

- Try to pronounce all the words correctly.

- Change your voice so that you read with expression.

> Suddenly, a fierce storm blew up and it looked as though the boat might sink.
>
> Then Jean and his friends saw a strange knight rising out of the waves.
>
> The knight shouted, "You nearly killed the dolphin king, and for this you'll all drown!"

5 Answer the questions.

a Name two characters in this story.

_____   _____

b Tick the phrases that describe the setting of the story.

☐ a long time ago   ☐ at sea

☐ in a castle   ☐ near France

c What happened before the storm? Tick the true sentence.

☐ The knight took Jean under the water.

☐ Jean threw a spear that hit a dolphin.

d Where does the knight live?

_____

e Who do you think the knight is?

_____

f Write a sentence that explains why there was a sudden storm.

_____

> Look at and think about each of the *I can* statements. ☐

Date: _____

1 Write a word to name each picture.

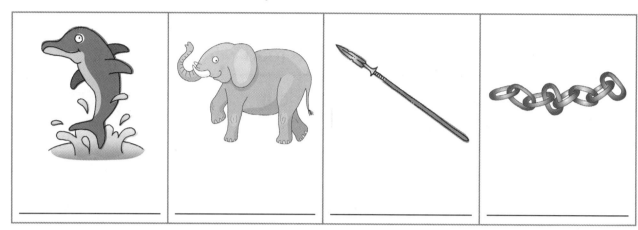

_____   _____   _____   _____

2 Read each word aloud and circle the suffix.

handful   useful   careful   helpful

3 🎧 Audio 8 Listen and write the sentences that you hear.

a _____

b _____

c _____

d _____

4 Write sentences about Jean in *The Dolphin King*. Use these words in your sentences.

• truthful

_____

_____

• promised

_____

_____

5 Write these sentences about *The Dolphin King* in the order in which they happened.

The dolphin screamed and dived under the water.

Jean promised not to hunt dolphins again.

The knight took Jean under the water.

A strange knight rose out of the water.

Jean hit a dolphin with his spear.

Jean helped to heal the dolphin king.

_____

_____

_____

_____

_____

_____

Look at and think about each of the *I can* statements.

Date: _____

1 Look at the pictures and read the texts. Is each picture or text fiction or non-fiction? Tick the correct box.

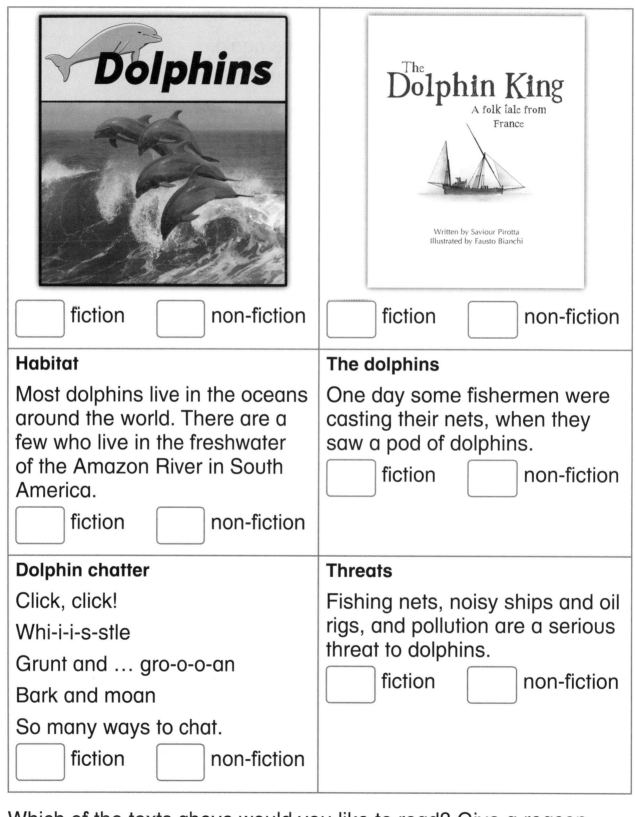

☐ fiction ☐ non-fiction | ☐ fiction ☐ non-fiction

Habitat

Most dolphins live in the oceans around the world. There are a few who live in the freshwater of the Amazon River in South America.

☐ fiction ☐ non-fiction

The dolphins

One day some fishermen were casting their nets, when they saw a pod of dolphins.

☐ fiction ☐ non-fiction

Dolphin chatter

Click, click!

Whi-i-i-s-stle

Grunt and … gro-o-o-an

Bark and moan

So many ways to chat.

☐ fiction ☐ non-fiction

Threats

Fishing nets, noisy ships and oil rigs, and pollution are a serious threat to dolphins.

☐ fiction ☐ non-fiction

2 Which of the texts above would you like to read? Give a reason.

c	s	w	a	v	e	s
x	t	j	k	l	m	n
d	o	l	p	h	i	n
p	r	o	m	i	s	e
z	m	q	u	s	g	p

3 Find four words from *The Dolphin King* in the word search puzzle.

4 Write the words you found in the word search puzzle in alphabetical order, with commas.

_____

5 Use these headings to plan a story about something that happened at sea.

Characters:

_____   _____   _____

Setting:

Time: _____

Where: _____

Weather: _____

Beginning of story:

_____

_____

Middle of story:

_____

_____

End of story:

_____

_____

6 Write your story in your notebook. Then correct it and read it aloud to a partner.

Look at and think about each of the *I can* statements.

Date: _____

1 Read the contents page.

> ### Frog or Toad?
> Written by Sue Barraclough
>
> **Contents**
>
> | | |
> |---|---|
> | Eggs | 2 |
> | Tadpoles | 4 |
> | Moving around | 6 |
> | Skin | 8 |
> | Food | 10 |
> | Other animals | 12 |

2 Answer the questions.

   a What is the title of the book? _____

   b What kind of book is it? Circle the correct answer.

      information (non-fiction)   a story

   c Who wrote the book? _____

   d What will you find out about on page 4? _____

   e On which page will you find out about what frogs and

      toads eat? _____

3 Complete the sentences using the words in the box.

   swarms   venom   sting   jaws

   a A funnel-web spider has _____ in its fangs.

   b Tiger sharks have very strong teeth and _____.

   c Deathstalker scorpions _____ with their tails.

   d Killer bees fly together in _____.

4 Read the information.

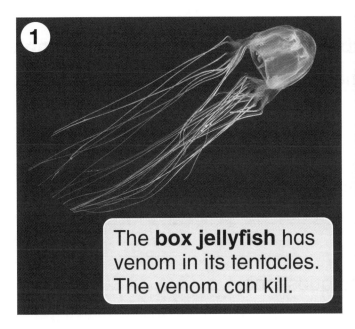

The **box jellyfish** has venom in its tentacles. The venom can kill.

The **golden poison dart frog** is deadly to eat or even touch.

5 Answer the questions.

Picture 1

a Why is the jellyfish deadly?

_____

b Which parts of the jellyfish are dangerous?

_____

Picture 2

a What colour is the frog?

_____

b Why is this frog so dangerous?

_____

Look at and think about each of the *I can* statements.

Date: _____

1 Write the words to show the syllables. Then count the syllables in each word.

Word	Syllables	Number of syllables
animal	a/ni/mal	3
spider		
octopus		
January		
September		
starfish		

2 Read the chart to answer the questions.

Where animals live

	On land	In water
bees	✓	
sharks		✓
lions	✓	
scorpions	✓	
dolphins		✓
tiger	✓	
swans		✓

a Where do bees and scorpions live?

_____

b Where do sharks and dolphins live?

_____

c Do lions live in water or on land?

_____

d True or false? Tigers live on land.

_____

3   Read the text silently.

> We should always treat animals with respect as they may hurt us if we bother them.
>
> Wild animals can be dangerous to humans. Lions, tigers, hippos, elephants and buffalo are big and strong. They can also move very fast. Some animals have big, sharp teeth or horns.
>
> Farm animals are not dangerous if they are treated well. Sheep, cows and rabbits are gentle creatures.

4   Use the information from the text and your own ideas to make lists of animals.

Animals

Dangerous	Not dangerous

5   Choose an animal from your lists.

- Draw a picture of the animal.

- Write three sentences about it.

- Then present your animal to others.

Date: _____

Look at and think about each of the *I can* statements.

49

1 Find words in the word search puzzle. Circle and then write the words.

t	e	a	c	h	c
f	l	o	w	e	r
z	z	x	y	a	o
w	q	z	x	d	w
e	d	t	j	q	r
a	p	e	a	c	h
r	x	a	g	k	h
t	h	r	e	a	d

a Two words that rhyme with 'beach':

_____   _____

b Two words that rhyme with 'bread':

_____   _____

c Two words that rhyme with 'pear':

_____   _____

d Two words that name the pictures:

i

ii

_____   _____

2 Rewrite the sentences. Add capital letters and a full stop or a question mark.

a i read my new book last night

_____

b is july before or after june

_____

c a scorpion stings with its tail

_____

d where can we find jellyfish

_____

3 Talk about the dangers in the pictures and complete the sentences.

a _____ because you can burn yourself.

b If you walk across a railway line _____.

4 Draw a picture of something else that is dangerous. Write two sentences to explain the danger in your picture. Tell a partner about the danger.

_____

_____

Look at and think about each of the *I can* statements.

Date: _____

Term 2 Test

1 Read the contents page and answer the questions.

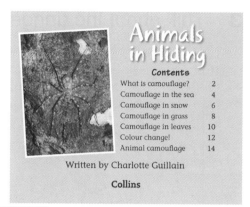

Animals in Hiding

Contents

Written by Charlotte Guillain

Collins

a Write the page numbers on which you can find the information.

   i What the word 'camouflage' means. ☐

   ii Can animals change colour? ☐

   iii How can animals hide in the snow? ☐

b What information can you find on page 4?

2 Read the text from *Animals in Hiding* silently.

What is camouflage?
Animals use camouflage to hide. Camouflage makes animals look like the place where they hide.

Some animals use camouflage to hunt other animals. Other animals use camouflage to hide from hunters!

Camouflage in the sea
Stonefish look like rocks. They hide to catch other fish.

Flatfish look like the seabed. They hide from bigger fish and sharks in the sand.

Camouflage in snow
A polar bear's white fur looks like snow. It can hide as it hunts.

This baby seal's white fur hides it from polar bears in the snow.

3 Answer the questions.

a Tick the sentences that are true.

☐ Animals use camouflage to hide from other animals and hunters.

☐ Animals use camouflage to play in the snow and sea.

☐ Animals use camouflage to hunt other animals.

b How does a stonefish camouflage itself?

_____

c Why does a flatfish camouflage itself?

_____

d Why are animals that live in the snow white?

_____

e What do polar bears hunt?

_____

4 What does this chart show about camouflage? Talk about the chart.

5 Complete this chart.

Animals that use camouflage

	To hunt	To hide
polar bear	✓	
baby seal		
stonefish		
flatfish		

6 Complete the compound words.

_____ fish   _____ fish

7 Add the missing syllables to these names of months.

__ /pril   Ju/ __   __ /vem/ber

8 Circle two words in each row that rhyme with the word in the first column.

white	light	bite	street
pair	pear	dear	hair
head	red	bead	bread

9 Complete the sentences. Use words from the box.

dislike   waves   unlock   fluffy   deadly

a The dolphins are playing in the _____.

b Some spiders have _____ venom in their fangs.

c Do you have a key to _____ this door?

d The clouds are _____ and white today.

e I _____ swimming because I don't like to get my hair wet.

10 Choose the correct word to complete each sentence.

a You should be _____ when you ride your bike on the street. (careful/care)

b We made a fruit salad with oranges and _____. (pairs/pears)

c Don't touch that frog _____ it may be poisonous. (because/but)

d The dolphin screamed and _____ under the water. (dived/diving)

11 Write a review of a book you have read this term. Use this form.

Title

_____

Name of the writer

_____

Type of book (fiction or information)

_____

Why I liked or did not like the book

_____

_____

_____

My favourite part of the book

_____

_____

_____

Look at and think about each of the _I can_ statements.

Date: _____

1   Read aloud part of the story poem *If*.

If you can play at baseball with a cheetah
who, fast as lightning, runs from base to base
and even though you know you'll never beat her,
you somehow keep a smile on your face.

2   Circle the correct answers.

a Which word rhymes with 'base'?

face   cheetah

b Who is 'her' in the sentence 'you'll never beat her'?

a cheetah   a crocodile

c Who can run faster, a cheetah or a boy?

a boy   a cheetah

d How does the boy feel?

He smiles bravely.   He cries sadly.

3   Write the words in alphabetical order.

alligator   hippo   dinosaur   rhino   cheetah

4 🎧 Write the sentences that you hear.
Audio 9

a _____

b _____

c _____

d _____

5 Talk about these sentences with a partner and then complete them.

- If you are kind to other people, they may _____.

- If you shout at other people, they may _____.

- Everyone can be a monster sometimes, but _____.

6 Choose the correct word to complete each sentence.

a They walked _____ up the street. (slow, slowly)

b We had a _____ holiday at the beach. (wonder, wonderful)

c The boys shouted _____ as they played a game. (loud, loudly)

d Be _____! That water is very deep and dangerous. (careful, careless)

7 Write sentences using two of the words from the box.

friendly   quickly   nicely

_____

_____

Look at and think about each of the *I can* statements.

Date: _____

1 Underline the adjective in each sentence.

   a This is the biggest dinosaur in the museum.

   b The greedy hippo ate my bread.

   c The angry rhinos are grunting.

   d An elephant is stronger than a giraffe.

2 Underline the nouns in the sentences from the poem *If*.

   a If you can play at baseball with a cheetah

   b If you can cross the playground in the morning

3 Write the verbs in the correct form. Add *-s*, *-ed* or *-ing* to the root word.

   a What are you _____ now? (do)

   b Last night we _____ a film about spaceships. (watch)

   c My sister _____ football for the town team. (play)

   d A cheetah _____ very fast. (run)

4 🎧 Write the sentences that you hear.
Audio 10

   a _____

   b _____

   c _____

   d _____

5 Choose the correct word to complete each sentence.

a I am _____ than my best friend. (smaller, small)

b We _____ a game of baseball yesterday. (playing, played)

c The people are _____ away because they are afraid. (running, runs)

d Last night was the _____ night of the year! I was frozen. (coldest, colder)

e She _____ when she doesn't win. (shouts, shouting)

6 Write your own poem. Change the underlined words in the verse.

If you can <u>watch</u> a spaceship landing
and when the others <u>run away</u> in fright,
you treat the <u>strange</u> green <u>men</u> with understanding
and though they're <u>rude</u>, you are still polite …

If you can _____ a spaceship landing

and when the others _____ in fright,

you treat the _____ green _____

with understanding

and though they're _____, you are still polite …

Look at and think about each of the *I can* statements.

Date: _____

1 Read the words aloud.

> December   gentle   mice   goldfish
> giraffe   danger   cereal   cake

2 Read the words aloud. Write the words that rhyme in the correct lists.

> base   do   two   case   polite
> night   fright   shoe   race

face	sight	you

3 Join a sentence from each column to make five longer sentences. Join the sentences with 'and', 'but' or 'because'.

I saw an alligator
You can race against a cheetah
They all went to the park
Some people stared
Sam was afraid

you will not beat it.
they wanted to play.
she saw a dinosaur in the park.
I saw some rhinos.
others ran away.

_____

_____

_____

_____

4 Use the form to plan an interview with someone. You will use the information to write a news report. You can interview the person about something special that they have done or seen.

Questions to ask	Answers
What _____ _____	_____ _____
Who _____ _____	_____ _____
When _____ _____	_____ _____
Where _____ _____	_____ _____
How did it end?	_____ _____

5 Plan a report about your interview in your notebook. Use these headings in your plan:

Headline   Beginning   Middle part   Ending

6 Write the report in your notebook. Then correct it and read it aloud to a partner.

Look at and think about each of the *I can* statements.

Date: _____

1 Read part of the story *The Pot of Gold* aloud.

Sandy and Bonny kept sheep.

"Too many sheep," said Bonny.

"Not enough sheep," said Sandy.

The two of them were always arguing.

"Can I stay here for two nights?" he asked.

"Yes," said Sandy.

"No," said Bonny.

"I can pay," said the little man. He took two gold coins out of his pocket.

"Well?" he asked. "Can I stay?"

One evening, they were busy arguing when there was a tap at the door. There on the doorstep stood a little man. He wore a green hat and a ragged green coat. His green shoes had holes in the toes.

"Yes!" said Sandy and Bonny. For once they agreed about something.

They took him to his room.

"Good night, and good luck!" said the little man. Bonny laughed. "We never have any luck," she said. But she was wrong.

2   Answer the questions.

a Who are the main characters in the story?

_____   _____   _____

b Which words describe the setting of the story? Circle two words.

evening   morning   sheep farm   town

c What did each character say? Complete the sentences.

> We never have any luck.   Can I stay here for two nights?
> Not enough sheep.

"_____" said the little man.

"_____" said Sandy.

"_____" said Bonny.

d Write two adjectives that describe the little man's clothes.

_____   _____

e Why did Sandy and Bonny stop arguing?

_____

3 Make a new character who knocks on Bonny and Bobby's door. Draw a picture and write labels to describe your character. Use different adjectives from the ones in the story.

Date: _____

Look at and think about each of the *I can* statements.

1 Number the pictures 1–9 to put them in the correct order. Then retell the story of *The Pot of Gold* to a partner.

2 Use these words to make three compound words.

market   one   bell   door   super   some

_____   _____   _____

3 Write the plural of each word. Then circle the plurals in the word search puzzle.

mouse _____

woman _____

tooth _____

foot _____

goose _____

person _____

w	o	m	e	n	a
h	g	i	f	e	p
a	e	c	e	f	n
l	t	e	e	t	h
k	c	b	t	t	w
g	e	e	s	e	t
p	e	o	p	l	e

4 Choose the correct word from the box to complete each sentence. Use each word once.

> and   if   or   but   because   when

a Sandy and Bonny looked every night _____ they didn't find the gold.

b "We can buy more sheep _____ we find the gold," said Sandy.

c Bonny picked up a jug of water _____ threw it over the little man.

d The little man was gone _____ they came home.

e Sandy was excited _____ he saw a heap of gold coins.

f We could buy a new house _____ we could buy some sheep.

5 Write two sentences that the character you drew on page 63 might say. Use direct speech.

" _____ "

" _____ "

> Look at and think about each of the *I can* statements.

Date: _____

1 Circle four nouns in these sentences that do not have plural forms.

They gave the man food and water.

Bonny wanted to buy some sheep with the gold.

2 Use the question words in the box to write questions about the story *The Pot of Gold*.

Tell a partner your answers.

Who	When	Where	Why	How	What

a _____ wanted more sheep?

b _____ did the little man knock on the door?

c _____ did Sandy put a stick in the pile of stones?

d _____ did Sandy find the gold coins?

e _____ did Sandy plan to get the coins back to the house?

f _____ did the old man do after Bonny threw water on him?

3 Write two questions of your own about the story.
Use question words.

_____

_____

_____

_____

4 Think about a story that you have read.

Plan a different ending for the story.

Tell your new story to a partner.

Discuss the story and improve it.

5 Write a description of a character from *The Pot of Gold*. You can choose Sandy, Bonny or the little man. Use some of the adjectives below to describe the character.

clever

funny

silly

quiet

bossy

grumpy

greedy   noisy

_____

_____

_____

_____

_____

_____

6 Act the character you have described.

Look at and think about each of the *I can* statements.

Date: _____

Fighting fires in Australia

Australia is a big country, with towns and cities as well as large areas of open land, bush and forests. The country is hot and dry, and **bushfires** are common in hot, windy weather. Fires kill many people and animals, and cause a lot of damage to property.

MAP OF AUSTRALIA

There are often big fires in the eastern part of Australia which has many **eucalyptus** forests.

a eucalyptus forest on fire

Small aeroplanes and helicopters are used to **waterbomb** fires.

Role of firefighters

Firefighters in Australia are trained to do many different tasks. They put out fires and save people and animals. They also give first aid to victims of fires. They always work in groups.

Firefighters wear special clothing to protect themselves against the fires. They spray water and chemical foam on fires to put them out. They use **fire trucks** with special equipment such as ladders and hoses.

Many of the firefighters in Australia are **volunteers** who are not paid to fight fires. They help every time there is a big fire.

1 Read the text on the previous page. What is it about?

_____

2 How do you know it is a non-fiction text?

_____

3 Find this information and make a list under each heading.

Firefighting equipment	The work of firefighters

4 Write these words in syllables and read them aloud. Then work out the meaning from the text.

eucalyptus eu/ca/lyp/tus   a type of tree

volunteer _____   _____

bushfire _____   _____

waterbomb _____   _____

firefighter _____   _____

5 Look at the map. Name two parts of Australia in which there are often big fires.

_____   _____

Look at and think about each of the *I can* statements.

Date: _____

1   Write down two compound words that have the word 'fire' in them.

_____   _____

2   Write the words to show the syllables. Then count the syllables in each word.

	Syllables	Number of syllables
forest		
firefighter		
helicopter		
equipment		

3   Complete the sentences about bushfires in Australia using the words in the box.

eucalyptus	bushfires	hot	burn

There are many _____ in Australia. The country is

big and it has large areas of bush as well as

_____ forests. The trees and grass

_____ easily when it is very _____

and windy.

4 Complete the sentences about firefighters using the words in the box.

save	trained	first aid	put out

Firefighters work in groups. They are _____ to do

many different tasks. They _____ fires and

_____ people and animals. They also give

_____ to victims of fires.

5 Share some information about fires with a partner.
Talk about:
- how fires start
- what you can do if you see a fire.

6 Write two sentences with important information about firefighting.

_____

_____

Look at and think about each of the *I can* statements.

Date: _____

1 Use the index to find the page where you will find the answers to the questions below.

Index

Bushfires	4, 7
Eucalyptus trees	4
Firehoses	8
First Aid	11
Helicopters	9
Protective clothing	10

a What does a eucalyptus tree look like?

_____

b What clothing do firefighters wear?

_____

c How do helicopters put out fires?

_____

d Where does the water for the firehose come from?

_____

2 Write these words in alphabetical order.

hose   siren   volunteer   waterbomb

_____

_____

_____

_____

3 Write the correct glossary definition next to each word in question 2.

dropping a lot of water from the air

a pipe or tube used for getting water to a fire

a loud sound that warns people of danger

someone who works without getting paid

4 Tick the sentences that are true.

Firefighters work as a team.	
There are no bushfires in Australia.	
Helicopters use hoses to spray water on fires.	
Firefighters wear helmets, gloves and other clothing to protect themselves from fires.	
Fire trucks carry firefighters and equipment to fires.	

5 Write two sentences about the work that firefighters do.

_____

_____

_____

_____

6 Imagine that you and your partner are firefighters. You get a call from someone at a shop to come and put out a fire. Role play the scene.

Look at and think about each of the *I can* statements.

Date: _____

1 Choose **one** of the following texts, A, B or C. Practise reading it aloud.

If you can keep your head when alligators are stealing all the bedclothes from your bed and keep your cool when, 15 minutes later, a greedy hippo eats your eggy bread …

The next day, Sandy was on the hill with the sheep when he saw a big pile of stones.

"That's funny," he said. "I can see something gleaming."

Sandy took away some of the stones, and he saw a heap of gold coins!

"I'll run home and fetch a big pot to carry them in," he said.

Firefighters use jet skis to put out fires on small boats. Jet skis work in shallow water.

Helicopters must fly in low.

The forests will grow again.

Fires spread quickly through forests. Helicopters water-bomb forest fires.

2 Make a presentation to a group.

- Explain what you are going to read and what it is about.

   Start like this:

   > I am going to read …
   >
   > It is about …

- Read the text aloud.
- Answer questions about the text.

3 Read these pages from the story *Bert the Ugly Bug* silently.

Bert the bug was feeling sad.
"I am such an ugly bug," he said.
"I look so dull and plain."
Bert sat in the dark and sighed.

2

Bert saw something bright coming towards him.
"I wish I was bright," said Bert.
He peeked out from under a leaf.

3

The frog did not see Bert. It jumped right past him.

It was a bright red frog. Bert stared at the frog.
"I wish I was bright like you," said Bert.
"I am such an ugly bug!"

4

Bert sighed and ran up the branch. He saw something glowing.

5

4 Answer the questions.

a Why was Bert feeling sad?

_____

b Where was Bert?

_____

c What did he wish? Copy a sentence from the story.

_____

d Why did the frog jump past Bert?

_____

e What do you think Bert saw that was 'glowing'?

_____

5 What do the underlined words in these sentences mean?

a "I look so dull and plain."

_____

b He peeked out from under a leaf.

_____

6 Read the end of the story silently.

7 Talk about these questions with a partner.

a Who is kind to Bert?

b How does this make Bert feel?

8 Write something kind that you could say to Bert. Start like this:

"Bert, you _____

_____."

Look at and think about each of the *I can* statements.

Date: _____

Acknowledgements

Text acknowledgements
The publishers gratefully acknowledge the permission granted to reproduce the copyright material in this book. Every effort has been made to trace copyright holders and to obtain their permission for the use of copyright material. The publishers will gladly receive any information enabling them to rectify any error or omission at the first opportunity.

Cover illustration: *Kind Emma* Reprinted by permission of HarperCollins*Publishers* Ltd © 2005 Martin Waddell, illustrated by David Roberts, *Jodie the Juggler* Reprinted by permission of HarperCollins*Publishers* Ltd © 2005 Vivian French, illustrated by Beccy Blake; *The Ugly Duckling* Reprinted by permission of HarperCollins*Publishers* Ltd © 2013 James Mayhew; *Hanako's Egg* Reprinted by permission of HarperCollins*Publishers* Ltd © 2021 Mio Debnam, illustrated by Yu Kito Lee; *Kind Emma* Reprinted by permission of HarperCollins*Publishers* Ltd © 2005 Martin Waddell, illustrated by David Roberts; *The Dolphin King* Reprinted by permission of HarperCollins*Publishers* Ltd © 2012 Saviour Pirotta, illustrated by Fausto Bianchi; *World's Deadliest Creatures* Reprinted by permission of HarperCollins*Publishers* © 2012 Anna Claybourne; *Animals In Hiding* Reprinted by permission of HarperCollins*Publishers* Ltd © 2013 Charlotte Guillain; *If* Reprinted by permission of HarperCollins*Publishers* Ltd © 2012 Mij Kelly, illustrated by Mark Beech; *The Pot of Gold* Reprinted by permission of HarperCollins*Publishers* Ltd ©2006 Julia Donaldson, illustrated by Sholto Walker; *Fire! Fire!* Reprinted by permission of HarperCollins*Publishers* Ltd © 2005 Maureen Haselhurst, illustrated by Chris Rothero; *Bert the Ugly Bug* Reprinted by permission of HarperCollins*Publishers* Ltd © 2013 Mal Peet and Elspeth Graham, illustrated by Simona Meisser.

We are grateful to the following for permission to reproduce copyright material:
Robert Charles Howard for the poem 'Dolphin Ballet', published in *Unity Tree: Collected Poems* by Robert Charles Howard, 2007, Createspace, copyright © Robert C. Howard.

Photo acknowledgements
The publishers gratefully acknowledge the permission granted to reproduce the copyright material in this book. Every effort has been made to trace copyright holders and to obtain their permission for the use of copyright material. The publishers will gladly receive any information enabling them to rectify any error or omission at the first opportunity.

P18tl Mjaud/Shutterstock; p18tr Ariful Azmi Usman/Shutterstock; p18bl A. RICARDO/Shutterstock; p18br A. RICARDO/Shutterstock; p22t Anastasiia Guseva/Shutterstock; p22ct Anastasiia Guseva; p22c Weha/Shutterstock; p22cb Olleg Visual Content/Shutterstock; p22b VectorforPro/Shutterstock; p29 Rudmer Zwerver/Shutterstock; p44 Willyam Bradberry/Shutterstock; p46t Eric Isselee/Shutterstock; p46b Eric Isselee/Shutterstock; p47l Visual&Written SL/Alamy Stock Photo; p47r imageBROKER/Alamy Stock photo; p50l Nadezhda F/Shutterstock; p50r Eric Isselee/Shutterstock; p52t Naturepl.com/Premaphotos; p52ctl David Chapman/Alamy Stock Photo; p52ctr Naturepl.com/Bert Willaert; p52cbl Reinhard Dirscherl/Alamy Stock Photo; p52cbr Blickwinkel/Alamy Stock Photo; p52bl WaterFrame/Alamy Stock Photo; p52br Minden Pictures/Alamy Stock Photo; p53tl SuperStock/Animals Animals; p53tc Jim Zuckerman/Alamy Stock Photo; p53bl Minden Pictures/Alamy Stock Photo; p53br SuperStock/Michel &Christine Denis-Huot/Biosphoto; p68t Maradaisy/Shutterstock; p68c Janelle Lugge/Shutterstock; p68b Cewington/Shutterstock; p70 Janelle Lugge/Shutterstock; p71l Tony Myers/FirepixInternational; p71r Isiah Shook/Shutterstock; p75t Tony Myers/FirepixInternational; p75c Reuters/Corbis; p75b Corbis/Ecoscene/Andrew Brown.